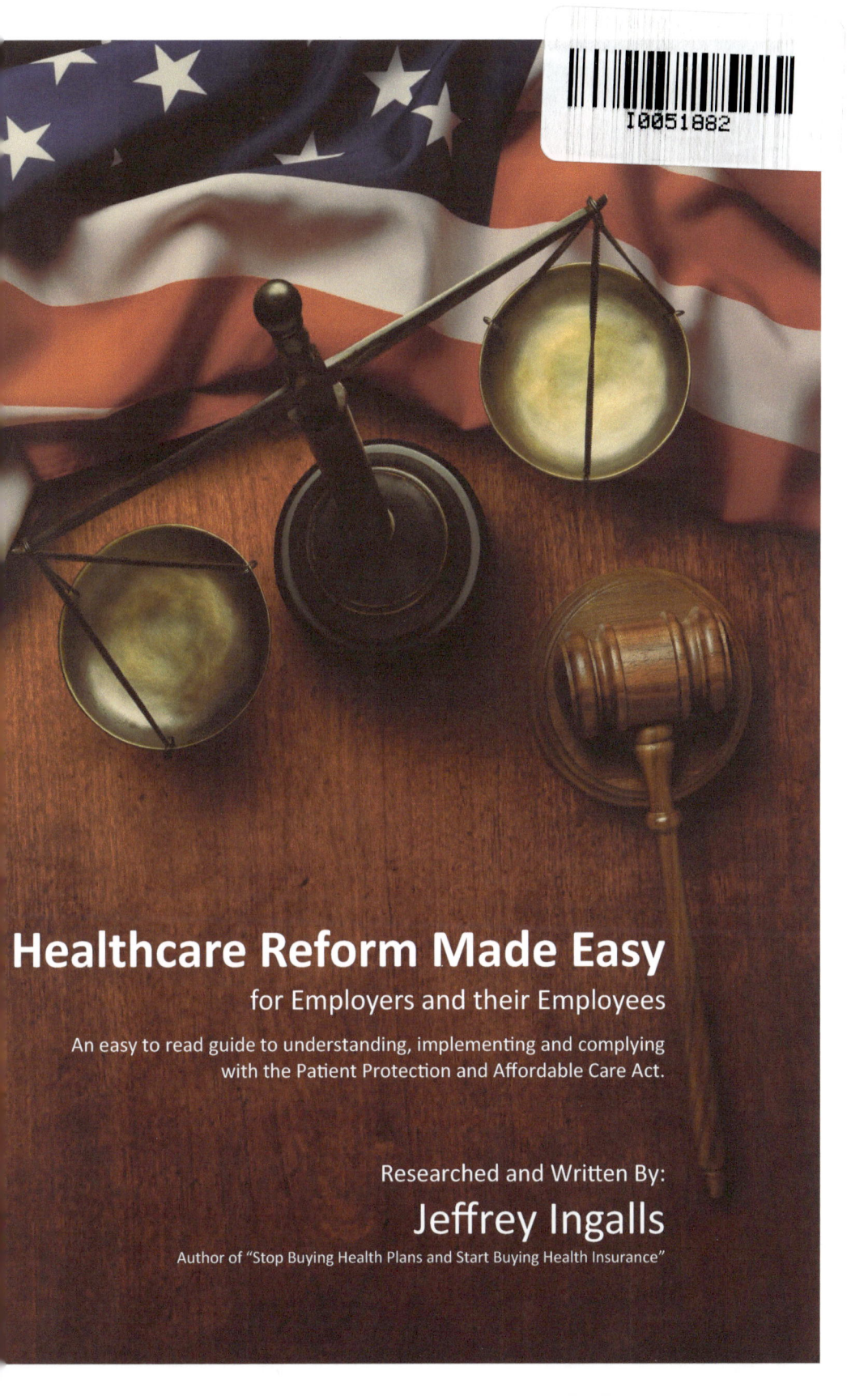

Healthcare Reform Made Easy

for Employers and their Employees

An easy to read guide to understanding, implementing and complying
with the Patient Protection and Affordable Care Act.

Researched and Written By:

Jeffrey Ingalls

Author of "Stop Buying Health Plans and Start Buying Health Insurance"

You are <u>60 minutes</u> away from understanding HEALTHCARE REFORM

About The Author

Jeffrey Ingalls is the President of The Stratford Financial Group and Stratford Employer Services located in Wayne, NJ. His previously published works include <u>Stop Buying Health Plans and Start Buying Health Insurance</u> authored in 2007. Jeffrey also hosted a weekly call-in radio program entitled "For Your Benefit" and has served as a guest speaker and industry expert at many events, symposiums and panel discussions across the state.

His television appearances include The Big Idea on CNBC and Simon Says, a local financial talk show. He is an industry expert for eHow.com with many videos concerning employee benefits and related topics. He is a contributor to Entrepreneur Magazine, Crain's, New York Enterprise Report, The Bergen Record and many other national and local newspapers and magazines.

Jeffrey is married to his wife Lisa and resides in Cedar Grove, NJ with his four boys: Atticus, Holden, Denham and Cash.

Jeffrey's contact information is listed below.
Employers, consumers and members of the media, feel free to contact him. He doesn't take days off, he works on weekends and is always accessible.

Toll Free: 866-217-9053 ext. 203
Cell Phone: 973-464-8050
Email: jingalls@stratfordlink.com
Company Website: www.stratfordlink.com
Blog: www.benefitsdr.com
Twitter: @benefitsdr

For purposes of writing this guide and communicating it's highly controversial subject matter, please note:

I am not a Republican. I am not a Democrat.
I do not own a coffee cup with the logos of FoxNews or MSNBC on it.
(I drink Starbucks out of their own biodegradable paper cups way too often.)
I don't watch Hardball or Hannity.
I am not an advocate nor an adversary of The Patient Protection and Affordable Care Act or healthcare reform.

I often refer to the legislation as healthcare reform quite frankly because it's easier than typing Patient Protection and Affordable Care Act a million times. And referring to it as PPACA is just plain annoying. Acronyms make things easier to say, not easier to understand. This is a complex law that I am attempting to make easy to understand. Acronyms, step aside.

I am not an Economist.
I am not a Political Scientist.
I am not an Accountant.
I do not work for the IRS.
I do not eat Green Eggs and Ham.
(Uncle) Sam, I am (not).

Things I am NOT.

I am a business owner...like you.
I am responsible for employee benefits...like you.
I am a healthcare consumer...like you.
I have not spent any time complaining or campaigning.
I have spent countless hours reading, researching, questioning and learning this law and its impact.

This guide is for business owners, human resource professionals, benefits administrators and healthcare consumers. It's not meant to be revolutionary. It's meant to make a very complex piece of legislation that's extremely difficult to understand...easy. Easy to understand, easy to implement and comply with for you and your employees. I guess what I am trying to say is...

When it comes to healthcare reform, what I care about most is how the Patient Protection and Affordable Care Act will effect my family, my company and my employees. I'm thinking that most business owners and those in charge of employee benefits at their company think the same way.

The problem is...
No one is talking about that! Doctor after doctor, lawyer after lawyer, expert after expert, no one writes about healthcare reform from the perspective of the employer. No one tells the business owner or the one in charge of employee benefits at a given company where they stand, what they need to do and the most important aspects of the law they should be focusing on now to prepare to comply with and implement healthcare reform, the Patient Protection and Affordable Care Act.

That is, until me. That is, until now.

I've been to seminars and symposiums on this subject and watched the so-called experts miscommunicate aspects of the law and respond to questions with statements such as, "formal guidance to follow." That's what I tell my kids when I am pretty sure what they're doing is wrong but I just don't know why.

I've seen employers ask simple questions like, "I have exactly fifty employees. Am I subject to the Employer Mandate?" and I've watched that employer leave without a simple answer to a yes/no question. I've seen another audience member ask a question about the small business tax credit and receive a response of, "You should consult with your accountant." He replied, "I am an accountant."

My goal is to include in this guide everything you need to know and not waste your time on the aspects you don't. Give me an hour and I will give you an unquestionable amount of value, answers to actual questions and the know-how to prepare to implement and comply with healthcare reform, as 'easily' as possible, at your company.

One last thing. I will not use 2,020 words when simply 20 will do. This book is meant to be easy to understand and respectful of your time, not wordy for the sake of being wordy.

Confession time. I don't have a crystal ball.

This book is intended to provide an easy to read guide that will allow you to understand healthcare reform and its impact specifically on your company and your employees. In doing so, this book will contain and offer guidance, based on the information available at the time it was printed, to allow you to be prepared to both implement and comply with the Patient Protection and Affordable Care Act. This landmark legislation continues to develop and evolve and its regulations are, in many cases, yet to be written or finalized. It is important to note that as the regulations are released, additional editions of this same publication will be released and the guidance contained may also change and be altered in response.

This is the First Edition of Healthcare Reform Made Easy
Published October 2012

The Patient Protection and Affordable Care Act...

stands over 9 inches tall, weighs 19 pounds, is 2,409 pages long and contains over 400,000 words. And that's just the law, never mind the Reconciliation Act, the Supreme Court decision, the guidance and the regulations. This guide is shorter, weighs less and includes far less pages and words. It is far easier to understand, though.

Table of Contents

Plan Administration

Included in Section One...

Five Different Definitions of an Employee

Excessive Waiting Periods

Variable Hour Employees

Summary of Benefits and Coverage

Automatic Enrollment Provision

W-2 Reporting Requirements

Flexible Spending Accounts

Five Different Definitions of an Employee

In the Patient Protection and Affordable Care Act, there are five different definitions of an employee. Each of the following aspects or provisions of the legislation, at the moment, defines an employee differently:

- Small Business Tax Credit
- Medical Loss Ratio (MLR)
- The Exchange (Small Health Options Program)
- Employer Mandate ("Play or Pay" Provision)
- Automatic Enrollment Provision

Don't worry, I'll explain each of these provisions later. For now, let's just get a handle on how an employee is defined.

You are in luck. I have all the definitions. Since I have all the definitions, my friends call me Webster. My friends are not that funny or creative. *(Author's Note: Get new friends.)*

Ok, now that one of my very few attempts at inserting humor into a guide about healthcare reform is out of the way, let's get started.

Ready?

Small Business Tax Credit

The Small Business Tax Credit provision became effective January 1, 2010. In order to be eligible for the tax credit, small employers offering a health insurance program need to meet three criteria. The first criteria for eligibility is the employer needs to have 25 or fewer full-time equivalent employees (FTEs).

Employers calculate the number of full-time equivalent employees by taking all the hours worked by employees during the calendar year and dividing by 2080, which is designed to represent a 40 hour workweek. This includes hours worked by full-time, part-time, terminated, seasonal employees (120 days or more) and employees of affiliated companies under the rules defined in Section 414 of the Internal Revenue Service (IRS) tax code.

Employers should exclude overtime hours for employees included in the count. They should also exclude all seasonal employees that were hired for a seasonal purpose (to work less than 120 days per year). Lastly, business owners, partners and their family members should also be excluded from the count. This includes:
- self-employed individuals, including sole proprietors and partners in a partnership;
- individuals owning more than 2% of a subchapter S corporation;
- individuals owning more than 5% of a corporation; and
- certain family members and dependents of these individuals such as children (or descendants of children), siblings or step-siblings, parents (or ancestors of parents), step-parents, nieces, nephews, aunts, uncles, sons-in-law, daughters-in-law, mothers-in-law, fathers-in-law, brothers-in-law, and sisters-in-law, and any member of the household of an owner or partner who qualifies as a dependent (as defined by IRS code).

To simplify the task of counting hours, employers are allowed to utilize any of the following methods of totaling hours worked:
- actual hours worked;
- include 8 hours for each day worked; or
- include 40 hours for each week worked.

Medical Loss Ratio (MLR) Market

The Medical Loss Ratio (MLR) provision became effective in the 2011 calendar year. Again, we will explain this provision later but for now, we need to discuss how to determine your market segment; in other words whether, according to this provision, your company is defined as small group or large group. The provision utilizes the Federal definition of an employee which means full-time, part-time and seasonal employees are all included. Even though this is information that is collected by your health insurance carrier, an employee's eligibility or enrollment in the health insurance plan is irrelevant to the calculation. Additionally, if your company is currently enrolled in a small group plan in your state's small group marketplace that does not necessarily mean you are in the small group market segment for purposes of the Medical Loss Ratio (MLR) provision.

The provision defines a small group as having 100 or fewer employees during the calendar year (not your health insurance plan year). Conversely, a large employer is defined as having 101 or more employees. Up until 2016, each individual state is allowed to define a small group as having 50 or fewer employees and large group as having 51 or more employees. For example, my home state of New Jersey elected to define a small group as having 50 or fewer employees.

Your fully-insured medical carrier will request this information from all employers sponsoring a health insurance program on an annual basis, typically in the first quarter.

The Exchange or Small Employer Health Options Program (SHOP) will be the venue whereby individuals and employers (initially, small employers) will be able to purchase coverage on January 1, 2014. Much like with other provisions, an eligible small employer is defined as an employer with 100 or fewer employees on business days in the preceding calendar year. Once again, each state does have the right to define a small employer as one having 50 or fewer employees until 2016.

When the legislation was written to create the national and state-level exchanges, a full-time employee was defined as one working 35 or more hours on a regular basis. Given the definition in the yet to be discussed provisions such as the Employer Mandate or "Play or Pay" provision, the excessive waiting period guidance and the safe harbor for variable hour employees, this provision's definition will likely be altered. It is likely the definition of a full-time employee will be set at 30 hours or more per week.

To further complicate matters, the Exchange will likely have its own participation requirements, definition of a valid waiver and has yet to rule on the continued eligibility and handling of employees working less than the designated full-time definition of 30 hours or more. For instance, small employer health insurance programs in New Jersey define full-time as working 25 or more hours on a regular basis. Will these employees continue to be deemed eligible? Will they be counted in the participation requirement?

Employer Mandate

The Employer Mandate (or "Play or Pay Provision") becomes effective on January 1, 2014. As I will repeat several times, the provision is not interested in when your company's health insurance program renews or your plan years starts or ends. This provision becomes effective on January 1, 2014. Employers subject to this provision are those that employed an average of at least 50 employees on business days in the preceding calendar year. In other words, your 2013 population will determine whether or not your company is subject to this provision in 2014.

To determine how many employees are at your company, you will need to look at your monthly population. Each employee working 30 or more hours per week counts as one employee. Next you will need to add up all the monthly hours worked by the balance of employees (the part-time employees or those working under 30 hours per week on a regular basis) and divide their cumulative monthly hours by 120 (soon to be amended by newer guidance to be 130). Add this number of full-time equivalent employees to the first number of actual full-time employees and you have your total number of employees.

It is important to note that employees of affiliated companies as defined under Section 414 of the Internal Revenue Service (IRS) tax code and Union or collectively bargained employees are included in the count. Seasonal employees hired exclusively to perform seasonal work and working less than 120 days per year are not included in the count. Leased employees or temporary employees, supplied by a temporary employment agency, are deemed to be working for the temporary agency or leasing company.

Automatic Enrollment Provision

The Automatic Enrollment Provision becomes effective on January 1, 2014; however, this is a provision that most experts agree will likely be delayed. This provision looks for employers with more than 200 employees.

This provision will likely be delayed because the regulations detailing who must be enrolled, into which plan and with what contact type have yet to be written. Additionally, the procedures and protocols associated with "opting-out" have also yet to be finalized and approved.

As it stands now, this provision leaves the definition of a full-time employee to the employer to define.

Obviously, this definition would need to be at least as high as the number of hours defined within the group health insurance contract itself or it may have adverse effects on an employer's ability to reach the participation requirement dictated by the health insurance program.

Additionally, there are obvious connections (I will point these out in the later sections) between this provision and other provisions such as the Employer Mandate which may result in a more "harmonious" definition of an employee being set at one working 30 or more hours on a regular basis.

Excessive Waiting Periods

As the law is written now, beginning with plan years starting on January 1, 2014 or later, employees cannot be forced to satisfy a waiting period that is longer than 90 days. I assume this provision will likely be interpreted to become effective exactly on January 1, 2014 regardless of your company health insurance program's plan year.

This means employers cannot utilize a waiting period of three months or "first of the month" following 90 days because this could result in a waiting period of 91 days or longer. Furthermore, waiting periods of "first of the month" following 60 days can still be problematic because an employee hired on June 1st would be made to wait 92 days before becoming effective on September 1st.

This provision is closely tied to an employee's individual Exchange eligibility and the tax penalties in the Employer Mandate. With that in mind, those employers with an excessive waiting period should either change their waiting period upon their 2013 renewal or as of January 1, 2014.

Employers should also note this provision may affect the administrative manner in which their chosen health insurer handles or issues mid-month enrollments, additions and changes and the corresponding premiums they bill. As a result, employers may need to change the manner in which they collect employee contributions via payroll deductions.

At this point in the guide, you should have a solid understanding of the many different definitions of a full-time employee in the various provisions of healthcare reform. So when your company hires a new employee or has an existing employee that works a set number of regular hours for which they are scheduled, calculating your number of employees is not necessarily easy but should be clear.

But what about variable hour employees, employees that do not work a set number of hours a week? Are they full-time or not? This is a question that will have unquestionable effects on the tax penalties levied under the Employer Mandate and your liability as an employer to make your health insurance benefits available to all full-time employees.

At least until the end of 2015, the Internal Revenue Service (IRS) has issued guidance that suggests the usage of the following safe harbor equation to define new or existing variable employees as full-time (or not). I am simplifying it here because I could probably write an entire book full of examples and pontification but remember this is supposed to be 'Healthcare Reform Made Easy" not Healthcare Reform Made Harder.

Step One—Develop a measurement period.
The measurement period, allowed to be between three and twelve months in length, is the period of time in which new or existing employees are tested to see if they have worked 30 or more hours per week, on average.

Step Two—Decide if you need to implement an administrative period.
The administrative period is a period of time allowed to be no more than 90 days in length. It is designed to provide employers time between the measurement period and the stability period to make the health insurance benefits available to newly defined full-time employees and complete the required paperwork and enrollment process.

Step Three—Administer a stability period.
The stability period is the period of time in which the determination of full-time status (or not) calculated during the measurement period has to last. The stability period is mandated to be at least six months or equal in length to the measurement period, whichever is longer. In other words, if your company decides upon a nine month measurement period then your company must also utilize a nine month stability period.

It is important to note that although some flexibility exists in your design of a measurement period, administrative period and the resulting stability period, a new employee defined as full-time cannot be made effective any later than the first of the month following 13 months from his or her hire date. In other words, a selection of a twelve month measurement period will directly affect the length of time available to utilize as an administrative period.

Employers need to perform this testing for both new employees and for existing employees. It is a good idea to set your existing employees' measurement period to end in the vicinity of your health insurance plan's open enrollment. This should eliminate the stress on your human resources and benefits staff to repeat open enrollment procedures for variable hour employees.

Step Four—Administer the transition from the new employee to existing employee testing.
During an employee's initial year of employment, there will likely be a period of time in which the testing or stability period as a new employee will overlap the testing or stability period of an existing employee. It is important to note that if a new employee is determined to be a full-time employee, that determination must last the entire duration of the stability period even if overlapping existing employee testing determines he or she to not be a full-time employee. Conversely, a new employee that is determined not to be a full-time employee based on the new employee testing will have that determination overruled if while in the stability period, the existing employee testing determines he or she to be a full-time employee.

Now would be a good time to take a deep breath.

Summary of Benefits and Coverage

The Summary of Benefits and Coverage (SBC) provision is effective on your first plan renewal subsequent to September 23, 2012. For most fully-insured group health insurance plans this is a provision with joint accountability between employers and their chosen health insurers. That, in my opinion, is a clever way of saying anything that goes wrong is the fault of the employer.

A Summary of Benefits and Coverage (SBC) is an eight page document (four double-sided pages to be exact) that is meant to uniformly describe benefits and enable consumers to easily compare plan benefits across all markets and available coverages. The document is heavily regulated right down to the font size. It must be available in English and four non-English languages as "linguistically appropriate" for your employee population (Spanish, Chinese, Tagalog, and Navajo). Your chosen health insurance carrier will provide the documents.

The document must be made available in paper form. Additionally, you cannot force an employee with whom you have never communicated with electronically, to communicate with you electronically for purposes of meeting the requirements outlined in this provision.

The Summary of Benefits and Coverage (SBC) must be provided at the following times or in the following circumstances:

- 30 days prior to your health plan renewal;
- during the open enrollment period (for all plan designs for which the employee is eligible);
- within 7 days after coverage is effective;
- within 7 days after a plan change is effective (group or member);
- within 7 days of a request;
- within 90 days of a special enrollment (loss of other coverage); and
- at least 60 days prior to a material modification of coverage (off-anniversary plan change or major benefit change)

Automatic Enrollment Provision

The Automatic Enrollment Provision becomes effective on January 1, 2014; however, as I mentioned earlier, this is a provision that most experts agree will likely be delayed. This provision is applicable to those employers with more than 200 employees.

As we discussed , this provision leaves the definition of a full-time employee to the employer to define. Given the glaring connections between this provision and other provisions such as the Employer Mandate, the end result will likely result in the definition of an employee being set at one working 30 or more hours on a regular basis.

This reasoning behind the likely delay is due to the fact that the regulations detailing who must be enrolled, into which plan and with what contract type have yet to be finalized and approved. In other words, there is no guidance dictating whether employers have to enroll employees in the lowest cost plan available or the plan available with the richest benefits.   Additionally, the procedures and protocols associated with "opting-out" of the automatic enrollment have yet to be finalized as well.

The W-2 Reporting Requirement becomes effective as of the 2012 taxable year and applies to the resulting W-2s to be issued in January of 2013. Only employers issuing more than 250 W-2s are subject to this provision. Unlike many other provisions, the rules defining affiliated companies found in Section 414 do not apply, at least during the transitional relief period governing the 2012 W-2s.

Employers need to report, for informational purposes only, the total cost of the health and pharmacy coverage inclusive of both the employer and employee contributions. They also need to report the cost of any employee assistance programs (EAP), wellness programs or on-site clinics assuming a COBRA premium is charged to continue with these coverages. Dental, Vision, Health Reimbursement Arrangement (HRA) and other group coverages are not included.

The administratively taxing aspect of this provision is that it forces employers to track coverage costs per employee and account for mid-year rate changes, plan changes, contract-type changes and coverage terminations and additions.

Those employers with self-insured health and pharmacy plans or reportable employee assistance and wellness plans will likely rely upon the COBRA equivalent premium method to determine reportable cost.

Flexible Spending Accounts (FSA)

The limitation on health Flexible Sending Account (FSA) contributions and salary reductions is effective as of plan years beginning January 1, 2013 or later. The limitation states that all elective employee contributions and salary reductions to a Flexible Spending Account (FSA) will be limited to a maximum of $2,500 per plan year.

Non-elective or employer contributions do not count towards the $2,500 limitation. Spouses, even if working for the same employer, are permitted to independently make a separate $2,500 contribution to his or her own health FSA. This limitation does not apply to a Health Reimbursement Arrangement (HRA) or Dependent Care Account (DCA).

Employers should, retroactively if need be, amend their plan documents to be in compliance with the newly mandated maximum. This will create needed revisions to the employer plan document, summary plan descriptions (SPD) and open enrollment materials.

The Exchange

Included in Section Two...
National and State-Level Exchanges
The Exchange Plan Designs
Small Health Options Program (SHOP)
Premium Assistance Subsidy
Cost Sharing Assistance Subsidy

National and State-Level Exchanges

Effective January 1, 2014, healthcare reform will create the American Health Benefit Exchange or national exchange and each state will have the opportunity to establish their own state-level exchange or participate in a federally-facilitated exchange.

The Exchanges are being created to improve and increase competition amongst insurers in the individual and small employer health insurance markets, improve the choices of affordable health insurance available to consumers and provide employers in the small group marketplace the same purchasing power as employers in the large group marketplace. The Exchanges will serve as an improved electronic marketplace to simplify the purchasing process insuring customers have all the tools and information required to make the best, educated decision for their coverage. The Exchange will also perform many of the administrative tasks soon to be required by other provisions of the legislation. Those responsibilities include certifying health plans as qualified health plans, determining individual and small employer eligibility for enrollment and determining and certifying eligibility for the Exchange-facilitated government assistance programs namely, the premium assistance subsidy and cost sharing assistance subsidy.

Each state is required to submit a blueprint for the creation of their state-level Exchange by November 16, 2012. At the time of this guide's printing, some states have submitted a blueprint but the majority were either considering or electing not to submit a blueprint. This will allow Health and Human Services (HHS) to approve the creation by January 1, 2013. The state will then embark upon creating their designed Exchange to be operational in time for the initial January 1, 2014 wave of enrollment.

As we will discuss in the sections to follow, the Exchanges are designed to provide qualified plans based on a very specific benefit requirements and rating criteria.

Effective January 1, 2014, both the national and state-level exchange will offer qualified plans to eligible individuals and small employers. A qualified plan is one that provides the ten essential health benefits, the limited cost-sharing dictated by healthcare reform and provides the minimum essential coverage with the actuarial equivalent of the Bronze, Silver, Gold or Platinum plans (also known as "The Metal Plans" as depicted below). Now let's take each of these characteristics one by one.

The ten essential health benefits include ambulatory patient services, emergency services, hospitalization, maternity and newborn care, mental health and substance abuse disorder services (including behavioral health treatment), prescription drugs, rehabilitative and habilitative services and devices, laboratory services, preventive and wellness services and chronic disease management, pediatric services (including oral and vision care). It is important to note that each plan cannot include a monetary lifetime or annual maximum of any of the ten essential benefits. The degree to which any essential benefit may be limited (such as an annual visit maximum) will be determined by the use of a benchmark plan to be selected by each state and approved by Health and Human Services (HHS).

Healthcare reform mandates certain cost-sharing limitations applicable to Exchange based plans as well. Annual deductibles will be limited to a maximum of $2,000 for single coverage and $4,000 for family coverage. This is a rather confusing provision as it does not yet spell out whether it applies to only deductible-first based programs, cost-sharing programs, in-network coverage, out-of-network coverage, etc. The other cost-sharing limitation refers to the maximum out-of-pocket which is

Bronze Plan	Silver Plan	Gold Plan	Platinum Plan
60%	70%	80%	90%

limited to the Internal Revenue Service (IRS) defined maximum currently relative to only High Deductible Health Plans or Health Savings Account qualified plans. In 2013, that limitation will be $6,250 for single coverage and $12,500 for family coverage. This limitation refers to out-of-pocket associated with all eligible expenses, inclusive of prescription drugs.

The last characteristic of a qualified plan is its actuarial equivalent. As the graphic on the previous page illustrates, the "metal plans" have the following actuarial equivalencies:

Bronze = 60%
Silver = 70%
Gold = 80%
Platinum = 90%

This does not mean these plans have no deductible, copays or varying co-insurance coverage levels of any kind. It does not mean that all eligible expenses are covered at 90%, 80%, 70% or 60% from day one. It does mean that if a standardized claims experience dataset was utilized (so all insurers' playing ground was even), the Bronze plan for example, would be expected to pay, on average, 60% of expenses for essential health benefits, and covered individuals, on average, would be expected to pay the remaining 40% in the form of deductibles, co-payments, and co-insurance.

The insurance carriers participating in the Exchange will include both the insurance carriers operating in your state as well as government sponsored programs.

Small Health Options Program (SHOP)

The Small Health Option Program or SHOP will become open for business (in other words, enrollment) within the Exchange on January 1, 2014. This program is designed to allow small employers to purchase group coverage through the Exchange. Coverage purchased will still be eligible for use with pre-tax contributions in conjunction with a valid Section 125 program. Initially (until 2017), an employer's eligibility for the Small Health Options Program (SHOP) is limited to small employers, defined as employing 100 or fewer employees. Once again, each state has the right to further restrict the definition of a small employer to 50 or fewer employees until 2016. Effective January 1, 2017, all employers will have access to group coverage through the Small Health Options Program (SHOP) .

All coverage available through the Small Health Options Program (SHOP) is guaranteed issue meaning carriers cannot deny coverage or even consider the medical history, profile or experience of a group when pricing or offering coverage. Coverage cannot be denied and is guaranteed renewable meaning it can not be cancelled because of medical experience related reasoning either.

Coverage is rated based upon plan selected and effective date. The only other variances are age and tobacco use. A 3 to 1 ratio for age is utilized meaning that the pricing for the least favorable age related risk (a 64 year old) cannot be priced at more than three times the cost of the most favorable age related risk (an 18 year old). Additionally, insurers can utilize a 1.5 to 1 ratio based upon tobacco use which would mean a tobacco-user or smoker would pay a premium that is 50% higher than a non-smoker. Gender (male or female) is not an allowable pricing variance.

For those employers with 50 or fewer employees, the state in which you are sitused would dictate whether or not these provisions would equate to a major difference in coverage pricing and availability. In my home state of New Jersey, for example, we will likely continue to set the definition of a small employer utilizing the 50 or fewer threshold. Within our current small employer marketplace, we already offer guaranteed issue and guaranteed renewable coverage, much of which already includes the ten essential health benefits and likely, the minimum essential coverage (actuarial value). It also currently priced utilizing a 3 to 1 ratio based on age. The differences between our current small employer marketplace and that of the Small Health Options Program's (SHOP) design would be the 1.5 to 1 ratio based on tobacco use and the disallowed use of gender as a pricing variance.

Also using New Jersey as an example, our current mid-size marketplace is defined as an employer having 51-99 employees. This is a marketplace where coverage is not necessarily priced upon an individual company's experience but regardless, coverage is manually rated and often carriers will decline to quote if they are uncomfortable with the risk or cannot compete with a inforce carrier's rates and benefits. If our state was to define a small employer at 100 or fewer employees, the Small Health Options Program (SHOP) would then equate to increased availability, namely carriers offering quotes that may result in improved pricing and increased benefit options for employers of this size.

Premium Assistance Subsidy

Effective January 1, 2014, individuals meeting certain eligibility and income criteria will be offered a Premium Assistance Subsidy. The subsidy is an advance tax credit only applicable to coverage purchased through the Exchange. An advance tax credit means the government will provide the subsidy funds to the Exchange who will in turn, administratively provide it to your chosen health insurer. A subsidy receiving individual will only need to pay their reduced premium as opposed to paying the full premium and taking a tax deduction at the end of the year.

If an individual is offered "affordable" minimum essential coverage (terms that I will define in greater detail in the sections to follow), he or she will not be eligible to purchase subsidized coverage through the Exchange. Assuming an individual is not offered affordable or minimum essential coverage through an employer and has a household income of between 100% and 400% of the Federal Poverty Level (FPL), he or she would be considered eligible for the Premium Assistance Subsidy. (Based on the 2012 Federal Poverty Level, individuals earning $44,680 and families of four earning $92,200 or less would be subsidy eligible.)

The Premium Assistance Subsidy is designed to set the annual premium relative to a percentage of the annual household income. Utilizing a sliding scale, annual premiums are set at a percentage rate of 2.0% to 9.5% of household income. The subsidy amount itself is based upon enrollment in the Silver plan; however, eligible individuals can utilize the subsidy amount towards a lesser priced Bronze plan or a higher priced Gold or Platinum plan.

The chart below illustrates the Premium Assistance Subsidy.

Premium Assistance Subsidy
Based on Silver Plan Premiums
(can be applied to any Exchange Plan Design)

Percentage of Federal Poverty Level	Annual Household Income (minimum)	Percentage of Annual Household Income	Annual Premium (rounded)	Monthly Premium (rounded)
100% to 132%	$11,170	2.0%	$223	$19
133% to 149%	$14,856	3.0% to 4.0%	$446	$37
150% to 199%	$16,755	4.0% to 6.33%	$670	$56
200% to 249%	$22,340	6.33% to 8.05%	$1,414	$118
250% to 299%	$27,925	8.05% to 9.05%	$2,248	$187
300% to 399%	$33,510	9.5%	$3,183	$265
400%	$44,680	9.5%	$4,245	$354

The Annual Household Income and Annual and Monthly Premiums illustrated above refer to the lowest percentage in each band of the Percentage of Federal Poverty Level column. For example, the percentage utilized in the 133% to 149% row is 133% and 3.0%

Cost Sharing Assistance Subsidy

Effective January 1, 2014, individuals meeting certain eligibility and income criteria will also be offered a Cost Sharing Assistance Subsidy. The subsidy affords eligible individuals who purchase Silver plan coverage through the Exchange to have the actuarial value of the Silver Plan increased and their maximum out of pocket reduced.

If an individual is offered "affordable" minimum essential coverage (terms that I will define in greater detail in the sections to follow), he or she will not be eligible to purchase subsidized coverage through the Exchange. Assuming an individual is not offered affordable or minimum essential coverage through an employer and has a household income of between 100% and 400% of the Federal Poverty Level (FPL), he or she would be considered eligible for the Cost Sharing Assistance Subsidy. (Based on the 2012 Federal Poverty Level, individuals earning $44,680 and families of four earning $92,200 or less would be subsidy eligible.)

The Cost Sharing Assistance Subsidy is designed to improve the Silver plan benefits in two ways. The first is to increase the actuarial value of the Silver Plan by reducing the enrollee's share of out-of-pocket costs which would likely result in some combination of reduced copays, deductibles and member coinsurance. The second is to reduce the Silver plan's maximum out-of-pocket.

Utilizing a sliding scale based on household income, the standard 70% actuarial value of the Silver plan is increased to a range between 73% and 94%. The Silver plan maximum out-of-pocket is reduced by two-thirds, one-half or one-third. This means the maximum out-of-pocket for single coverage of $6,250 could be reduced by as much as $3,125 per plan year.

The chart below illustrates the Cost Sharing Assistance Subsidy.

Cost Sharing Assistance Subsidy

Based on Silver Plan Enrollment

Percentage of Federal Poverty Level	Annual Household Income (minimum)	Silver Plan Actuarial Value	Maximum Out-of-Pocket Reduction
100% to 132%	$11,170	94%	2/3 Reduction
133% to 149%	$14,856	94%	2/3 Reduction
150% to 199%	$16,755	87%	2/3 Reduction
200% to 249%	$22,340	73%	1/2 Reduction
250% to 299%	$27,925	70%	1/2 Reduction
300% to 399%	$33,510	70%	1/3 Reduction
400%	$44,680	70%	1/3 Reduction

The Annual Household Income illustrated above refers to the lowest percentage in each band of the Percentage of Federal Poverty Level column. For example, the percentage utilized in the 133% to 149% row is 133%.

Employer "Shared Responsibility"

Included in Section Three...
Affordable Employee Contributions
including Safe Harbor for Affordability
Minimum Essential Coverage
including Essential Health Benefits and
Cost-Sharing Limitations

In the previous sections concerning the subsidies available for eligible individuals purchasing coverage through the Exchange, I repeatedly referred to employer-sponsored coverage being "affordable" and providing the minimum essential coverage. In these next two sections, I will explain and define each of these critically important components of healthcare reform for employers.   These two components are the only two factors determining whether or not eligible individuals can gain access to the available subsides (which are further based on household income) within the Exchange and whether or not employers subject to the Employer Mandate, based on size, will be subjected to tax penalties.

Subsequent to the passing of the Patient Protection and Affordable Care Act, the Internal Revenue Service (IRS) realized that it would be next to impossible for employers to be able to determine the household income of their employees. Realizing that basing this equation on an employee's income would be a much easier task, the Internal Revenue Service (IRS) created a safe harbor for employers to use to determine whether or not their health insurance plan offering is affordable.

The equation utilized by the safe harbor compares the annual W-2 wages in Box 1 for each employee to the annual single coverage contribution for the lowest cost qualified plan (a plan providing minimum essential coverage). If the annual contribution equates to 9.5% or less of income for every employee, then the employer has successfully created a safe harbor for affordability and would eliminate one of the two triggers determining:
- whether or not eligible individuals can gain access to the available subsides within the Exchange; and
- whether or not they, as the employer, would potentially be subject to the Employer Mandate tax penalties.

Please remember, this testing is not performed cumulatively or "on average" for your entire population but rather separately for each full-time, eligible employee working 30 hours or more per week on a regular basis. Additionally, this testing is performed at year end to confirm affordability for the year past but can also be used prospectively for the future year assuming employers will make the necessary mid-year adjustments to maintain the 9.5% or less wage requirement for each employee.

The creation of a safe harbor for affordability does create a challenge for the Exchange in the way of determining eligibility for your employees with dependents. Again, the creation of a safe harbor (and providing minimum essential coverage—to be discussed in the next section) would essentially negate your employees' eligibility for the Exchange subsidies but would also immunize your company from the tax penalties found in the Employer Mandate.

In regards to your employees with dependents, they may not qualify for the Exchange subsidies based upon employee income and the contribution and coverage relative to the employer-sponsored health insurance program; however, they may still qualify based on household income. This would likely mean either your employee could enroll with dependent coverage in the Exchange and receive the subsidies or just his dependents (spouse and children) could enroll in the Exchange and receive the subsidies. Both are possible but irrelevant to the employer and would not subject the employer to the Employer Mandate tax penalties. Providing affordable employer-sponsored minimum essential coverage will immunize those employers that are subject to the Employer Mandate and the tax penalties it will assess.

Minimum Essential Coverage

Once again, in the previous sections, I repeatedly referred to employer-sponsored coverage being required to provide minimum essential coverage. In this section, I will define this terminology as it relates to the two critically important components of healthcare reform for employers. A health insurance plan providing the minimum essential coverage means it has an actuarial value of 60% or greater. In other words, the plan benefits are as good or better than the Bronze plan offered in the Exchange.

The determination of actuarial value will commonly be performed in one of two ways. The first is the use of a minimum value calculator to be developed and provided by Health and Human Services (HHS) and the Internal Revenue Service (IRS). This will allow employers to examine certain standard cost-sharing attributes of their plan design such as co-payments, deductibles, co-insurance and out-of-pocket costs as they relate to four core categories of benefits including:

- physician and specialty care;
- hospital and emergency room services;
- pharmacy benefits; and
- laboratory and imaging services.

The calculator would also take into account employer contributions to a Health Savings Account (HSA) or funding available through a Health Reimbursement Arrangement (HRA).

The Internal Revenue Service (IRS) is also planning on releasing a safe harbor checklist to allow employers to determine whether or not their plan benefits in the four core categories exceed the minimums determined to be required to create the 60% minimum actuarial value of the Bronze Plan offered in the Exchange.

It is also assumed that the minimum essential coverage equation could be failed if the employer plan includes deductibles greater than $2,000 for single and $4,000 for family coverage or maximum out-of-pocket limits that are greater than those defined by the Internal Revenue Service (IRS) for high deductible or Health Savings Account (HSA) qualified health plans.

It is important to reiterate that minimum essential coverage for small employers would include the ten essential health benefits. This would equate to mandated coverage for ambulatory patient services, emergency services, hospitalization, maternity and newborn care, mental health and substance use disorder services (including behavioral health treatment), prescription drugs, rehabilitative and habilitative services and devices, laboratory services, preventive and wellness services and chronic disease management, pediatric services (including oral and vision care). All coverage for the ten essential benefits cannot include a monetary lifetime or annual maximum but may include other maximums or limitations (such as an annual visit maximum) as determined by the use of a benchmark plan to be selected by each state and approved by Health and Human Services (HHS).

Taxes and Credits and Rebates

Included in Section Four...

Patient Centered Outcome Research (PCOR) Fees

Small Business Tax Credit

Employer Mandate -"Play or Pay" Provision

Cadillac Tax

Medical Loss Ratio (MLR) Rebates

Patient Centered Outcome Research Fees

Healthcare reform has created a new non-profit corporation named the Patient-Centered Outcomes Research Institute in an effort to fund clinical effectiveness research. The creation of this organization will be fueled by fees ("PCOR fees") paid by certain health insurers and applicable sponsors of self-insured health plans, including employers offering a Health Reimbursement Arrangement (HRA). This provision is applicable to plans with plan years ending after September 23, 2012.

For fully-insured health insurance programs, the insurance carrier will pay the fee of $2.00 times the average number of covered lives under the policy or plan (the fee is $1.00 for plan years ending before October 1, 2013). For self-insured plans, the third party administrator (TPA) or plan administrator would need to calculate, report and pay the required fee.

There are special rules relative to counting the number of employees for Health Reimbursement Arrangements (HRA). In the case of an Health Reimbursement Arrangement (HRA), the plan sponsor is allowed to assume one covered life for each employee participating in the program. In other words, the plan sponsor is not required to count the number of covered spouses and dependents.

For those who have a fully-insured medical plan with an integrated Health Reimbursement Arrangement (HRA), the carrier will report and remit the fee. For those employers with a fully-insured health plan and a separate or stand-alone Health Reimbursement Arrangement (HRA), the employer must report and remit the fee.

Fees are to be reported and remitted once a year, even though they are reported on IRS Form 720, a quarterly Federal Excise Tax Return. Reports and payments for plan years that end in a calendar year are generally due by July 31st of the following year.

Small Business Tax Credit

The Small Business Tax Credit has been in effect since the 2010 taxable year. The intent of this provision is to provide a tax credit for those eligible small employers providing a health insurance program to their employees. To be deemed eligible for the credit, employers must satisfy three criteria.

The first criteria is the employer must employ 25 or fewer full-time equivalent employees (FTEs) during the calendar year. As we discussed, employers calculate the number of full-time equivalent employees by taking all the hours worked (except for overtime) by non-excludable employees that worked during the calendar year (including full-time, part-time, terminated, seasonal employees working 120 days or more and employees of affiliated companies) and divide by 2080. Employers should be careful to exclude hours worked by excludable employees such as business owners, partners and their family members.

The second eligibility criteria is that the salary provided for the hours worked by the non-excludable employees must maintain an average of $50,000 or less annually. This figure, unlike the calculation of hours worked, includes overtime pay.

The last requirement is that employers must make a uniform employer contribution towards the cost of the employer-sponsored health insurance coverage which is to say the employer must contribute at least 50% of the single rate.

The amount of the credit issued is a percentage of the employer's contribution to the premium and is based on a sliding scale that is greater for employers with less full-time equivalent employees and a lower average annual salary. Until 2014, the maximum amount of the credit is 35%, 25% for tax-exempt employers. In 2014, the maximum amount of the credit increases to 50%, 35% for tax-exempt employers; however, the credit is only applicable if coverage is purchased through the Exchange.

It is important to note that the amount of the tax credit will directly reduce the amount of employer premium contribution eligible for a tax deduction.

The complete sliding scale of the Small Business Tax Credit can be found below.

			Average wage			
Number of FTEs	$25,000 and less	$30,000	$35,000	$40,000	$45,000	$50,000
10 and fewer	35%	28%	21%	14%	7%	0%
11	33%	26%	19%	12%	5%	0%
12	30%	23%	16%	9%	2%	0%
13	28%	21%	14%	7%	0%	0%
14	26%	19%	12%	5%	0%	0%
15	23%	16%	9%	2%	0%	0%
16	21%	14%	7%	0%	0%	0%
17	19%	12%	5%	0%	0%	0%
18	16%	9%	2%	0%	0%	0%
19	14%	7%	0%	0%	0%	0%
20	12%	5%	0%	0%	0%	0%
21	9%	2%	0%	0%	0%	0%
22	7%	0%	0%	0%	0%	0%
23	5%	0%	0%	0%	0%	0%
24	2%	0%	0%	0%	0%	0%
25	0%	0%	0%	0%	0%	0%

Source: Congressional Research Service

Employer Mandate (Pay or Play Provision)

The Employer Mandate is probably the most talked about provision of the Patient Protection and Affordable Care Act or healthcare reform. It becomes effective on January 1, 2014 and will not coordinate with your health insurance program anniversary or renewal date. It begins on January 1, 2014, conveniently or not.

This provision is applicable to employers with at least 50 employees on business days in the preceding calendar year. In other words, it's your 2013 population that will determine whether or not your company is subject to the Employer Mandate in 2014.

Once again, to determine how many employees are at your company, you will need to look at your monthly population. Each employee working 30 or more hours per week on a regular basis counts as one employee. Next you will need to add up all the monthly hours worked by the balance of employees (the part-time employees or those working under 30 hours per week on a regular basis) and divide their cumulative monthly hours by 120 (soon to be changed to 130). Add this number of full-time equivalent employees to the first number of actual full-time employees and you have your total number of employees.

Once again, seasonal employees hired exclusively to perform seasonal work and working less than 120 days per year and leased and temporary agency employees are not included in the count. Conversely, Union or collectively bargained employees and employees of affiliated companies are included.

There are two tax penalties associated with the Employer Mandate. One tax penalty applies to those employers who do not offer coverage and the other applies to employers who offer coverage that is not deemed affordable or does not meet the minimum essential coverage requirement. The action that triggers either tax penalty is an employee deemed eligible for the subsidies electing to enroll in an Exchange plan and claiming the subsidies. There are no tax penalties unless this action takes place.

To emphasis this; unless one employee of a company is eligible and actually purchases coverage and receives the subsidy, no tax penalties are assessed.

If an eligible employee enrolls in an Exchange plan and does claim the subsidy and the employer does not offer coverage, the employer will be assessed a $2,000 annual tax penalty per employee minus the first 30 employees. It is important to note that the tax penalties are assessed monthly and will be imposed on all full-time employees working 30 hours or more, all variable hour employees deemed full-time and working within the stability period and all seasonal employees, even though seasonal employees were not included in the original count. Conversely, employers are not penalized on part-time employees even though they were utilized in the original count.

Employers that offer coverage that is either deemed unaffordable or does not meet the minimum essential coverage requirements will receive a $3,000 annual tax penalty per employee that is subsidized. Again, this is assessed monthly and applicable to all the employee classifications noted above. The maximum monthly tax penalty that can be assessed in this scenario cannot exceed 1/12th the sum total of $2,000 per employee minus the first 30 employees.

In the previous sections, I emphasized the employer's need to provide affordable minimum essential coverage. In doing so, employers can immunize themselves from any and all of the Employer Mandate tax penalties. In this same regard, employers should review the affordability and actuarial value of their current health insurance program offering. Employers may need to offer a richer or lesser health benefits plan in order to afford themselves the opportunity to successfully create the affordability and minimum essential coverage safe harbors.

Employers should also consider that the tax treatment of a $2,000 or $3,000 employer contribution to an employee's annual premium has a very different financial impact than a $2,000 or $3,000 non-deductible tax penalty.

Premium Excise or "Cadillac" Tax

The Premium Excise or "Cadillac Tax" is a highly discussed provision in healthcare reform probably because of it's easily recognizable nickname and the misconceptions surrounding it.

Beginning January 1, 2018, this provision provides for an excise tax to be placed on annual premiums in excess of $10,200 for single coverage and $27,500 for family coverage. That equates to monthly premiums of $850 for single coverage and $2,292 for family coverage.

The amount that is subject to the 40% excise tax are the amounts over the aforementioned premiums. The tax is levied on the employer-sponsored plan policyholder but collected and remitted by the insurance carrier. In essence, the insurance carrier acts as the collection agent.

It is my opinion that for most small employer programs, the insurance carriers will remove the plans in their portfolio that produce premiums above the designated thresholds rather than have to administratively deal with this taxable provision.

Medical Loss Ratio (MLR) Rebates

The Medical Loss Ratio (MLR) provision has been in effect since the 2011 calendar year. This provision forces fully-insured health insurers to spend set percentages, depending on your market segment, of every premium dollar collected on certain expenses, most notably claims.

Small group market employers are defined as having 100 or fewer employees and large group market employers are defined as having 101 or more employees. As we discussed previously, this employee count includes all employees: full-time, part-time, seasonal, everyone. It tallies employees on business days in the preceding calendar year regardless of their work status or eligibility or enrollment in the employer sponsored health insurance program. Once again, until 2016 states have the right to adjust the determining threshold between the small group market and large group market to 50 employees.

The small group market is held to an 80% medical loss ratio (MLR) and the large group market is held to an 85% medical loss ratio (MLR). The medical loss ratio itself is based on the following equation: Premiums collected minus certain taxes and regulatory fees divided by paid claims and the costs of quality improvement programs (for example, disease management programs).

Any overages above and beyond the 80% or 85% loss ratio must be rebated to the plan sponsor or in most cases, the employer. The carriers will typically collect the preceding year's employee count information during the first few months of the calendar year. By June 1st, insurers will then file with Health and Human Services (HHS) as to whether or not each of their market segments will be issuing a rebate and if so, how much. By August 1st, rebates are issued proportionally to the plan sponsors or employers based upon the enrollment of each employer group in the market segment.

Assuming employees contributed to the cost of the health insurance premium, the rebates received by the employer are deemed plan assets by the regulations of ERISA and must be handled and distributed in a very specific fashion and according to a very stringent set of rules.

The first item of concern is whether the employees contributed to the health insurance premium on a pre-tax or post-tax basis. If the employees contributed their portion of the premiums on a pre-tax basis under a cafeteria or Section 125 plan, rebates distributed as a reduction of future employee contributions to premium or in cash to employees will be subject to federal income tax in the year of distribution. Conversely, if employees paid their portion of the premiums on an after-tax basis, rebates that are distributed as a reduction of future employee contributions or in cash to employees will generally not be subject to federal income tax.

The rebates may be issued in cash, can be used for benefit enhancements (addition of coverage not previously inforce) or most often, a reduction in future employee contributions. All rebates must be distributed within 90 days or held in trust by the employer.

Employers are allowed to distribute the proportionate amount of the rebate to the employee population based either on the employee population that was insured during the timeframe on which the rebate was based or amongst the currently enrolled population. The ultimate goal is for the employer to employ a reasonable, fair and objective allocation method. Most employers have elected to refund to the currently enrolled population.

The rebates need to be distributed in a manner proportionate to the employee contribution for each plan offered. This would mean the rebate needs to be separated into the portion applicable to the employer's premium contribution and that which is applicable to the employees' contributions.

Some guidance relative to the most common employee contribution structures can be found below:
- If the employer pays 100% of the premium then no portion of the rebate is attributable to the employees.
- If the premiums are shared based upon a set, split percentage, then the rebate will be split based upon the same percentage.

- If the employer pays a set amount towards the premium and the employees' pay the overage, then the rebate is considered to be 100% attributable to the employees unless the rebate amount is greater than the sum total of the employees' contributions.
- If the employee pays a set amount towards the premium and the employer pays the overage, then the rebate is considered to be 100% attributable to the employer unless the rebate amount is greater than the total of the employer's contribution.

Often, the best and most prudent method of allocation is to distribute the rebate to the current plan participants by providing a reduction to the employee contribution in the month or months immediately subsequent to the receipt of the rebate.

Subsequent to 2012, it is also important to note that plan participants will receive a notice from their insurance carrier only when a rebate is being issued. With that in mind, it is possible for a health insurance plan to receive a renewal increase forcing the employer to raise employee contributions in a market segment that has received a medical loss ratio (MLR) rebate. In this scenario, employees would receive an increase to their required employee contribution and a medical loss ratio (MLR) notice from their insurance carrier basically stating "we made too much money so we're giving some of it back." With that in mind, it is important to educate employees concerning this provision to attempt to avoid unsettling conversations, born of confusion, in the future.

Other Information

Included in Section Five...

Individual Mandate
Non-Discrimination Testing
Simple Cafeteria Plans
Reinsurance Fees and Risk Controls
The Health Insurance Tax or "HIT"
Accountable Care Organizations (ACOs)

Beginning January 1, 2014, the Individual Mandate will levy a "shared responsibility" tax penalty on taxpaying citizens for any month that they, their spouse or their dependents do not maintain minimum essential coverage (as described in the Employer "Shared Responsibility' section).

In speaking of individuals and their coverage as opposed to employer-sponsored health plans, it is important to note that the requirement of maintaining minimum essential coverage could include the following:

- coverage under an employer sponsored plan;
- a government-sponsored program such as Medicare Part A, Medicaid, the Children's Health Insurance Program (CHIP) and TRICARE;
- an individual health plan available in the individual market; or
- any other health insurance program properly recognized by Health and Human Services (HHS).

The Individual Mandate tax penalty is assessed per month at a rate of 1/12 of the greater of two amounts—the "flat dollar amount" and the "percentage of income amount." The tax penalty does contain a maximum tax liability equal to the national average of the annual bronze plan premium, for the relative family size and contract type, offered through the state-level Exchanges

The annual "flat dollar amount" is phased in over three years and is applicable to each individual, spouse, or dependent that is without minimum essential coverage. The amount is set at $95 for 2014; $325 for 2015; and $695 in 2016 and thereafter. The amount for individuals age 18 or younger is half of the amount of the parent. The fixed amount for any individual is capped at three times the annual flat dollar amount per year, regardless of the number of individuals in the taxpayer's household who actually lack minimum essential coverage during the year.

The "percentage of income amount" is determined by first subtracting the taxpayer's exemption (or exemptions for a married couple) and standard deductions from the taxpayer's household income. The balance of household income is then multiplied by the following percentages: 1% for 2014, 2% for 2015, and 2.5% thereafter.

The Individual mandate does include exceptions for certain individuals including:
- specific religious conscience objectors;
- members of a health care sharing ministry;
- individuals who are not citizens, nationals, or an alien lawfully present in the United States; and
- incarcerated individuals.

Additionally, certain individuals are exempt from the tax penalty including:
- individuals who cannot afford coverage (individuals for whom coverage would cost more than 8% of their household income);
- individuals whose household income does not meet the required threshold for filing a federal income tax return;
- members of certain Indian tribes;
- individuals who have a gap in coverage for less than a continuous three-month period (this exemption may only be used once per year); and
- individuals who are issued a hardship exemption by Health and Human Services (HHS)

Healthcare reform imposes non-discrimination rules on fully-insured group health plans similar to those already in place for self-funded health plans. In general, the non-discrimination rules refer to preventing discrimination in the forms of eligibility and benefits offered and provided. This provision was originally slated to be applied to fully-insured health insurance programs' plan years beginning on or after September 23, 2010. It has since been delayed until at least January 1, 2014 allowing the applicable agencies sufficient time to produce further regulations and additional formal guidance.

The provision utilizes two common nondiscrimination tests—the Eligibility Test and the Benefits Test.

The Eligibility Test seeks to determine if a plan benefits one of the following groups of employees:
- 70% or more of all non-excludable employees;
- 80% or more of all non-excludable employees who are eligible to benefit, if 70% or more of all non-excludable employees are eligible to participate under the plan; or
- a nondiscriminatory classification of employees (this requires a legitimate business classification that clearly benefits non-highly compensated individuals).

In running the Eligibility Test, an employer may exclude from consideration employees who have not completed three years of service, are less than 25 years old, are part-time or seasonal, are collectively bargained, or are nonresident aliens who do not receive United States sourced earned income.

The Benefits Test seeks to confirm that all benefits provided to the highly compensated individuals (HCI) who are participating in the plan are also provided to all other participants. There are two subsections of this test known as non-discriminatory benefits on the face of the plan and non-discriminatory benefits in operation. (Keep in mind, the rules of affiliated companies as defined in Section 414 are applicable to this testing.)

A Highly Compensated Individual (HCI) is defined as follows:

- one of the five highest-paid officers;
- a shareholder who owns more than 10% of the stock; or
- one of the highest-paid 25% of all employees (other than excludable employees who are not participants).

In conclusion, employers should be certain that all classes of employees are being offered the same level of benefits, being asked to contribute the same (key employees can no longer receive better benefits without contributing) and being required to satisfy the same waiting period. Additionally, employers should be careful not to structure their health insurance offerings and employee contributions in a way that would cause only highly compensated individuals (HCI) to enroll in a plan. This could be deemed a failure of the subsection of the Benefits Test (non-discriminatory benefits in operation).

Lastly, the non-discrimination testing may also force small employers who are not subject to Employer Mandate tax penalties to not purposely or otherwise structure their health plan offerings or employee contributions to incent (or at least, enable) employees to receive the subsidies available in the Exchange. Not only is it still a question whether or not such employees would constitute a legitimate waiver, the exodus of the lesser compensated employees may cause the remaining highly compensated employees' enrollment in the health insurance plan to fail the non-discrimination testing.

Effective on January 1, 2011, healthcare reform allows eligible, small employers to establish a new type of cafeteria plan referred to as a "simple cafeteria plan". These plans will be deemed to meet the non-discrimination testing for cafeteria plans, namely Section 125 plans for pre-tax employee contributions assuming the following employer-size, contribution, eligibility and participation requirements are met.

The criteria for eligibility are as follows:
- The employer must have employed 100 or fewer employees on business days in either of the two preceding years. The rules regarding affiliated companies and Section 414 of the Internal Revenue Service (IRS) tax code are applicable to this provision.
- All employees who worked a minimum of 1,000 hours in the previous plan year must be eligible to participate in the plan. Each eligible employee must be eligible to choose any offered health insurance benefit plan.
- Employees who are not highly compensated employees (HCE) or key employees must receive employer contributions equal to at least 2% of the employee's plan year compensation or the lesser of 6% of the employee's plan year compensation or twice the employee's contribution.

Highly compensated employees are defined as:
- a more than 5% shareholder in the current or preceding plan year; or
- an employee that received compensation of more than $110,000 in the preceding plan year.

Key employees are defined as:
- an officer of the company with annual compensation over $160,000;
- a more than 5% owner; or
- a more than 1% owner with annual compensation over $150,000.

Employers may elect to exclude the following employees:
- those under the age of 21 before the end of the plan year;
- those with less than a maximum of one year of service;

- Union or collectively bargained employees; or
- certain non-resident aliens working outside the United States.

A small employer cafeteria plan that allows employees to make pre-tax contributions to the employer-sponsored group insurance plans and provides access to a Flexible Spending Account (FSA) and Dependent Care Account (DCA) would require to the small employer to perform and pass nine different discrimination tests. The simple cafeteria plan provision intends to simplify the process and remove much of the required testing.

Healthcare Reform creates three programs designed to eliminate incentives for health insurance carriers to avoid insuring high-risk and costly members. In other words, those who are in poor health. They are also designed to eliminate or avoid drastic swings in premiums from one carrier to the next and drastic increases in renewals from one year to the next. The three programs are known as the temporary reinsurance program and the risk corridor and risk adjustment provisions.

Effective January 1, 2014, each state is required to establish a temporary reinsurance program for the individual market for the period of 2014 through 2016. Every health insurance carrier, group health plan and third party administrator, on behalf of self-funded health plans, are required to contribute fees to fund this provision starting January 15, 2014. The provision or program is designed to stabilize the individual market that will likely explode with enrollment in 2014, given the available subsidies and other incentives. More specifically, the fees collected fund reinsurance costs for the individual market to shift the costs of high-risk claimants from the insurance carrier to the reinsurance carrier. The fees are expected to raise the annual cost of healthcare by $50 to $90 per member.

The risk corridor program is overseen by the federal government, namely Health and Human Services (HHS) and is initially temporary and designed to run from 2014 to 2016. This provision will be implemented to protect insurance carriers from having to charge premium rates for qualified health plans in the Exchange (individual and Small Health Options Program) at a higher rate than assumingly necessary to protect against the uncertainty of their claims experience. (Keep in mind, they can no longer use medical history or claims experience in setting initial rates or developing renewal rates.) These risk corridors are temporary (2014-2016) and are based on a formula that compares actual claims incurred and paid versus the "target" or expected claims expenses.

The risk adjustment provision is a permanent program created by healthcare reform and administered by the government. The purpose of the program is to distribute the risk or poor claims experience amongst the health insurance carriers participating in the Exchange. This will guarantee stability amongst each health insurance carrier's premiums regardless of the claims experience they actually incur, good or bad. In essence, the program provides payment to health insurance carriers that insure high-risk, large claim producing members by transferring funds from plans with best claims experience to the plans with the worst claims experience. Once again, this provision or program will reduce, if not eliminate, premium differences amongst plans based on good or bad claims experience within the individual and small group marketplace. All group health insurance plans are subject to this provision, both inside and outside of the Exchange.

The Health Insurance Tax or "HIT"

Effective January 1, 2014, each fully-insured health insurance carrier will be imposed a health insurance tax or "HIT" tax as it has become commonly known.

The aggregate annual fee for all fully-insured health insurance members is $8 billion for the calendar year of 2014, $11.3 billion for years 2015 and 2016, $13.9 billion for 2017 and $14.3 billion for 2018. Subsequent to 2018, the applicable amount will be determined based upon an indexed amount relative to the rate of increased premium and fully-insured membership.

The aggregate annual fee is distributed to each fully-insured insurance carrier in direct proportion to the amount of fully-insured members they insure. At the time of this publication, most experts agree that this tax will increase the annual premium of a family coverage by $400 to $500.

Accountable Care Organizations (ACO)

An Accountable Care Organization (ACO) is, by functional design, a new, more refined, closer-knit, technologically advanced version of the Health Maintenance Organization (HMO). An Accountable Care Organization (ACO) is a geographically based grouping of physicians, a hospital or hospitals and associated providers, such as laboratories and home health care providers. These providers work together and share information for the technologically supported, coordinated care of a patient in anticipation of improved, less costly outcomes.

This model of care serves to improve health care in the following areas:
- communication amongst physicians, hospitals, laboratories and other participating providers;
- quality of care and patient health outcomes;
- availability of a patient's full medical history, including testing and test results available to all participating ACO providers;
- reduced need for forms and medical history documentation
- reduction of unnecessary, repetitive tests; and
- more stable or lowered healthcare costs.

An Accountable Care Organization (ACO) could exist within the following health insurance plan settings:
- in a passive way (behind the scenes and embedded) in the in-network side of a managed care plan such as a Point of Service (POS) or Health Maintenance Organization (HMO)
- as an increased level of in-network care and benefit (think of a POS or HMO with two sets of in-network benefits– one for the ACO providers and one for the HMO providers)
- as the in-network participating providers in a POS setting (all other providers would be deemed subject to the out-of-network benefits).

Many Accountable Care Organizations (ACO) are already operational in a passive way for fully-insured health insurance programs.

What You Need To Do Now

Included in Section Six...

Healthcare Reform Preparation Checklist
How Stratford Can Help
What We Need To Get Started
How The Right Payroll Vendor Can Help

Healthcare Reform Preparation Checklist

As we stated, many provisions of the Patient Protection and affordable Care Act take effect on January 1, 2014 which means many employers will need to plan now to make changes in conjunction with their 2013 renewal.

1. Determine your company's number of employees based upon each provision and the varied definitions and methods for calculating.

2. If your company employs variable hour employees, create a safe harbor by determining the timeframe and measurement, administrative and stability periods that would be most advantageous to your goals (for example, deferring or diminishing your Employer Mandate tax penalty).

3. Review your employee waiting period. If changes need to be made, they need to be made in conjunction with your 2013 renewal as some carriers may not allow a mid-year change (assuming your plan does not renew January 1st).

4. Obtain the Summary of Benefits and Coverage (SBC) for your current health insurance plans. Determine the best protocol and delivery system to obtain compliance with the required distribution.

5. Review your company's eligibility for the Small Business Tax Credit, beginning back in 2010. Don't forget to exclude owners and their dependents from the calculations.

6. Review your employee contributions. Annualize the employee contribution needed for single coverage on your lowest priced plan, assuming it will meet the minimum essential coverage requirement. Forecast the contribution structure or plan design changes you may need to implement on your 2013 renewal.

7. Apply what you now know about minimum essential coverage and essential health benefits and make an educated assumption as to your plan's actuarial value. The calculators and safe harbor checklist to formally determine your plan's actuarial value in relation to the minimum essential coverage requirement should be available in the first quarter of 2013.

8. Small employers should determine if their current plan design includes all of the ten minimum essential benefits. If your plan does not include them or if any one of them currently contains a monetary annual or lifetime limit, be prepared for an increase in

2014.

9. Review your current plan design to determine if the deductible and maximum out-of-pocket amounts are greater than the maximum allowable amounts in 2014. Consider implementing a Health Reimbursement Arrangement (HRA) as a method to lower the amounts rather than changing your plan design and increasing the premium.

10. Consult with a healthcare reform expert or a knowledgeable employee benefits consultant and determine how the pricing variances used for premium development in the Exchange differ from those currently used in your state and market segment. Determine whether or not the Exchange may result in increased options and more advantageous, less costly pricing.

11. Determine how many employees, based on annual W-2 income will be eligible for the Premium Assistance or Cost Sharing Assistance subsidies. Remember that it is an employee deemed eligible who purchases coverage and claims the subsidy that triggers all the tax penalties in the Employer Mandate. This determination will prove to be important for future benefit and renewal planning.

12. If you do not currently offer coverage or you offer coverage that may be deemed unaffordable or failing the minimum essential coverage requirement, apply the Employer Mandate tax penalties to your current employee population to determine it's financial scope.

13. Even though the Cadillac Tax provision does not become effective until 2018, review your current premiums, make an educated assumption as to year-over-year renewal percentage increases and determine if this is likely a provision of concern for the future.

14. All employers will be required to complete a Medical Loss Ratio (MLR) form provided by your insurer so that they may collect employee population data to determine your market segment. Develop access to an Medical Loss Ratio (MLR) calculator to utilize if and when a Medical Loss Ratio (MLR) rebate is issued by your insurer in your state and market segment. During your next open enrollment season, prepare to communicate and educate eligible employees as to this provision.

15. Consult with your payroll vendor as to the number of W-2s to be issued relative to 2012. Develop the means and protocol required to track the newly required, reportable premium information.

We offer a *customized* **Healthcare Reform Made Easy IMPACT Report** with answers and solutions specific to your company and your employees.

The Healthcare Reform Made Easy IMPACT Report includes:

- Specific information and results relative to the mandates and provisions discussed in Healthcare Reform Made Easy
- Customized guidance relative to each of the fifteen points noted in the Healthcare Reform Preparation Checklist.
- Tailored healthcare reform consulting upon the delivery of the report as well as 90 days prior to your 2013 renewal.

The Healthcare Reform Made Easy IMPACT Report (and all its included deliverables) **costs:**

- We provide the report and the consultation as one of our standard service deliverables to our clients. It's a no-cost component of our already robust value proposition.
- We charge a one-time refundable fee to prospective clients. Become a client and we will waive the fee. For company specific pricing, please email: jingalls@stratfordlink.com

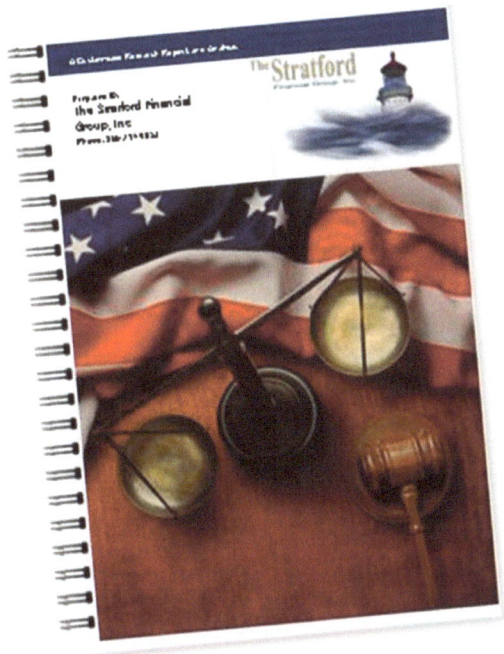

What We Need To Get Started

Listed below is the benefit plan and employee census information we need to obtain in order to prepare a **Healthcare Reform Made Easy** customized research report and analysis specific to your company and your employees.

Benefit Plan Information

Please include the information for each of medical/pharmacy plan designs offered.

- Summary of Benefits
- Employee and Employer Contribution Amounts
- Monthly Premiums
- New Employee Waiting Period

Employee Census Listing

Please include all employees (not only plan participants) including: full-time, part-time, union/non-union and seasonal.

- Employee Name
- Gender
- Date of Birth
- Annual Salary (not salary for a specified time frame)
- Hours Worked Per Week (on a regular basis)
- Date of Hire
- Designate all Owners and Employee Relatives
- Current Medical/Pharmacy Plan Section and Contract Type (if enrolled)
- Smoker / Non- Smoker Designation (if known)

How The Right Payroll Vendor Can Help

Think about it.
No one is positioned to track your employees better than your payroll vendor. No one communicates with your employees more than your payroll vendor - every cycle, another opportunity to communicate.

Why not utilize the position and line of communication of your payroll vendor to help rescue your time from the grasp of healthcare reform and all of its administrative calculations, reporting and notice requirements?

Stratford Employer Services have teamed up to create a payroll solution that automates as much of the tasks associated with healthcare reform as possible.
The Medial Loss Ratio (MLR) Report? Automated.
The NJ Small Employer Certification? Automated.
Summary of Benefits and Coverage distribution? Automated.

See how payroll can help you today.
Contact Mike Fornarotto at mfornarotto@stratfordlink.com

Stratford
Financial Group, Inc
Employer Services, LLC